Songs of Recovery

K. Olsen

Published by K. Olsen, 2024.

SONGS OF RECOVERY

First edition. June 26, 2024.

Copyright © 2024 K. Olsen.

ISBN: 979-8227360014

Written by K. Olsen.

Table of Contents

For everyone I have ever met along the way who shares or shared even a portion of these experiences. You are all wonderful and deserve the world. Don't let anyone tell you differently.

The Shelter of Thorns

No one asks the rose why it has thorns,
nor honey bees why they wield a sting,
nor oysters why they wrap pearls around pain.
All these things exist in nature,
not as malice, but the result of circumstance,
and so surely it follows:
it is natural to wish for safety.

So why do we scorn people for their boundaries
or tell them they are unreasonable,
when anger walls away their hurt?
Why tell ourselves that we are ugly
for our scars and our defenses
rather than seeing the brambles for what they are:
a consequence of all the little nicks and cuts,
a tool against the dangers we have known,
the opalescent shield we coat threats in?

We should remember too, the beauty here
is not in spite of the harsher parts;
instead, it is sheltered and completed by them.
Not: a rose, but wreathed in sharp brambles—
Instead: a bloom uplifted by its thorns.
Not: a sweetness, but with a venomed sting—

Instead: a diligent guardian of the hive.
Not: a pearl, but inside lies the ugly grit—
Instead: beauty crafted from suffering.

We are roses and honeybees and oysters
making our way in the world,
and so we should make space to understand
the shelter of thorns, the protection of stings,
and remember that even pain and hurt
can be healed by surrounding with growth—
without guilt or shame.

SONGS OF RECOVERY

For us, as all things, it is natural to wish for safety.

The Fire of Optimism

While some paint me as fragile as an autumn leaf
crunching underfoot on a wind-swept path,
I am more than the glow of a candle's flicker
or a sand-castle constructed below the tideline.

I am the ax inside the case of glass
beneath the stencil, "Break in case of emergency!"
I am the torch handed from future to present
illuminating darkness in a flood of fire.

I am the warmth suffusing frostbitten hearts,
the very essence of what it is to be alive.
Within you, I am the animus of change,
the flowing Life from which all breath comes.

I am more than the winning lottery ticket,
the card proclaiming, "Get out of jail free!"
I am the call to action, the promise of better,
coming when there is work to be done.

I am the pull unsatisfied by half-hearted pushes.
I do not simply tell you the grass grows greener:
I am the hose watering your own lawn.

So whether a lifeline or the hammer used
to construct the foundations of a better world:
hold me so tightly that there is no difference
between me, the calling tool, and your fingers,
for the closer Hope sits in your heart
the more room you have to grow.

For C—

I have stood where you stand now,
and I recall how fragile and afraid I felt,
as if poised on the edge of tearing in half.

But if you feel the same, I hope that you know
it is not brute force and hardness
that carries a butterfly thousands of miles
in migration across a wonderful world,
but the fragility of amber wings,
so delicate they too seem easily torn,
yet they ride winds like fluttering jewels:
a beautiful endurance and graceful learning
how to use even storming weathers
to reach their far-flung destinations.

They come from such humble beginnings,
yet are transfigured and reborn,
not through ease, but difficult work in a chrysalis,
into Monarchs, queens of the sky.

I hope you keep that vulnerability,
that gentleness, that sensitivity,
like amber wings inside your heart
and let them carry you

to exactly where you're supposed to be.

Life with ED

Indescribable from the inside,
inconceivable from the outside,
yet those who stand around pointing
claim to know its inscrutable depths
without having stepped even in shallows.

Allow me, then, the fish,
to describe an ocean:
its sighted, tossing waves
and unseen undercurrents.

The sharpness of a face with eyes like mirrors,
and cheeks hollow from imposed famine—
The brittleness of hair and nails,
stripped of their strength and shine—
The washboard ribs that jut beneath stretched skin—
A concave stomach that no longer aches,
because it has forgotten what fullness was—
Hips protruding like a skeleton's—
Painful knobs of knees and elbows—
The deprivation of wasted flesh and sallow skin,
wearing their pain more boldly than clothes—
The lumps of vertebrae lining down a back,
carrying hardships like Sisyphus's stone—

SONGS OF RECOVERY

All of this you see and call it vanity.

The heart that labors as it weakens,
stripped brutally of its strength until no more—
The bones that sacrifice their integrity,
until they are as fragile as a bird's.
The organs that struggle just to stay alive:
the liver, the kidneys, every piece
you healthy ones do not even think of,
holding the fraying body together—
Why? you ask. Why do this to yourself?
If you want part of your answer, turn to the mind:
first outside, then inside, as we shape the lens.

Anxiety picks and plays at uneaten food—
obsession chains to a cruel reflection—
You see insecurities swallowed with hurt
and all too often, no secrets come spilling out.
They show themselves as constant concern,
the shaping and modeling of presentation:
a perfect porcelain mask to hide the cracks.
Never saying what is felt, but instead,
this paltry voice squeaks what you wish to hear—
Never admitting the fish is drowning in its bowl,
slowly and steadily overcome by each gulp—You see distance,
preoccupation with appearance,
and presume the shallowness of it all,
not knowing that every grasp for control,
every gasp for breath, every body check,
is a symptom of a pain unfathomably deep.

Inside, there is the trauma collected
over years of cutting words and isolation,
some holding attacks as dark as starless night.
The uncertainties and distrust in the self
and the knowledge the world is not a place
where the mind feels safe or at home—
It is crammed into the darkest recesses,
where it spreads like choking vines,
digging twisted roots of guilt and shame
into every aspect of emotion and perception.
Just as the eye cannot see itself,
but trusts the lens to show it the world:
so too the fish relies on distorting water,
and presumes its failure upon twisted reflections
showing every imperfection cut to pieces
and magnified to endless size.
The refrain: If you are not perfection,
you should not exist, you should cease to be.

So where, you ask, does this leave the soul?
Surely nothing so sensitive could flourish
among the strangling vines.

Somehow yet it lives, constricted on all sides,
but yearning for freedom, thirsting for meaning.
The vines you see have dug themselves in deep,
but there is more than skin and bone,
more than anxiety, pain, and grief.
It exists among all the darkness as a light,

flickering, perhaps, and fragile as an eggshell—
It craves all the same things that you might:
comfort, safety, truth, love, healing, purpose,
the connection to what it is to be human,
and all these things are denied it
by the twisting coercion of the disorder.
And yet, it will never surrender hope for them,
no matter how far the reach or high the climb,
and there is a grief so potent it cannot be spoken
when it is forced to move on.

Please remember that your words are stones,
and stones cast into water send forth ripples:
some rocks churn up sediment and shadow
sending the fish deeper into the bowl,
while more thoughtful stones dropped with care
are a gentle disruption of the water and its lens,
allowing clarity and an awareness of beyond.

A Hope of Water

In you, I see all the strength and vitality of water:
the life-bringer whose currents stir beauty into the world,
sensitive to all the cycles of this ever-changing universe—
the gentleness of falling rain drops paired
with the power of the crashing wave focused upon a rock—
the free flow of ideas and inspiration,
channeled into beautiful purpose, but never truly caged—
indestructible and transfiguring.

I hope you take comfort in this:
no matter how tempestuous the storm, the waves are
unharmed—
no matter how high the dam, it allows flow or perishes—
no matter how hard the gemstone, water cuts it with the right
focus.

Water knows itself in any shape, elemental to its being,
and I know you will flow as freely as rivers course to sea,
chasing the meanings and passions you have found,
even if the course is winding and difficult.

A Hope of Fire

In you, I see all the brilliance and glow of fire:
the illumination of hope and life even in the darkest places,
a light to ward away evil and draw close safety—
protective in its flames and guiding in its sparks,
both hunger for the joys of life and a safe place to share them,
with no need to doubt itself, or the warmth it can offer—
burning with such intensity and passion,
it is both an implacable and beautiful thing.

I hope you take comfort in this:
no matter how dim and difficult things seem, coals can be rekindled—
no matter how difficult people say it is, fire is majesty itself—
no matter how icy the world, you can melt a way through it.

Fire knows itself in any shape, elemental to its being,
and I know you will burn with awe-inspiring brightness
to carry yourself and those you care for out of dark times,
even if sometimes the flames scorch the ground.

A Hope of Earth

In you, I see all the resilience and steadfastness of earth:
the sheer awe-striking power of great canyons' sight,
and the humbleness of the soil that gives a home
to every poet's glimpse of inspiring leaf and flower—
the humor that grounds all things in what they truly are—
with the endurance to persist when all the world is change,
for earth is not stone alone: it is sand, it is rock, it is clay, it is
metal—
the foundation of every deed and accomplishment.

I hope you take comfort in this:
no matter how the pressure increases, you will only become
stronger—
no matter how intense the fires you face, you will only reshape
the world—
no matter how large your problems seem, your endurance is even
more vast.

Earth knows itself in any shape, elemental to its being,
and I know you will thrive through it grounded in yourself,
in the steadiness and crystalline growth of rediscovery,
even though things may churn or quake.

Angels of a Better Nature

I have been blessed by angels,
who do not see the full measure
of the better nature they awaken in me.
Their words fall gentle as spring rain
on the parched and blistered earth
burned over by self-inflicted agonies.
Their touch is softer than owl feathers,
yet I see their fingerprints on my soul
as if imprinted into stone.

The goodness in people is seldom spoken,
and too often fades from view,
but never is it wholly gone:
instead, it echoes into eternity.

These angels of a better nature
have borne wingless me up
until I could see for myself
the reflection of their mercy in me,
the worth of a human being,
and the flowers born of every thorn.
They rekindled my compassion,
holding the pieces of my heart together,
so I could stitch them whole

with needle and thread they placed
into my hands with every lesson.

Wherever you go, there are angels:
hiding in the sublime imperfections of others.
Should you seek them out,
I wish you my good fortune in finding them,
so you might stand in the light
cast by their halos yourself.
The only thing they ask of you
is to pass on the gifts they give,
as they have done before you
in the names of their own angels.

The goodness in people is seldom spoken,
and too often fades from view,
but never is it wholly gone:
instead, it echoes into eternity.

Meditation on a Pinecone

After a raging fire has scoured the woods to nothing,
how does vivacious green know to return?
Hidden in cones cracked open by the flame,
what tells the pine seed it is safe?

For the storms and fires that rage in hearts
are no more gentle than the infernos
surging across summer slopes in drought,
leaving the ashes of forests in their wake.

What difference, the devastation of dreams,
the very rendering down to cinders,
of possibility, of future, of hopes, of self—
that so agonizing Grief of the Gaps?

Does Nature tell the seed when it is time,
or does it dare so greatly never knowing?

Perhaps there is no secret in the cues
seemingly so impenetrably mysterious to us,
the thinking, self-critical intersections
of falling angels and rising apes.

Perhaps safety is no more guaranteed

for the burgeoning pine than for the people
who look upon them with marveling eyes,
but an unconscious hope that guides them on.

Perhaps the self-same hope of change and life,
we then delude ourselves from with stories
of "this will never change" or "this is who I am",
as if anything is immune from metamorphosis.

What would happen if we changed the story,
drawing no border between our senses of self
and the ever ardent regrowth we witness flourishing year after
year before our eyes?

I think we would find another intersection
between what we have been, who we are,
and the heights of what we can be in time.

Cutting Words

I hope every curving stroke of this pen,
every deliberate line slashed across the page,
cuts your tongue like a razor blade,
so you might feel the vinegar sting
of the sour lies you tell through smiling lips.

The harm you have done to this place,
once a bastion of love, safety, and healing,
leaves a sickness of the soul in its wake,
like a poison droplet spreading in a clear pool.

It hurts me so, this outpouring of venom,
because it twists and shatters the very bonds
of trust holding all righteous things in place.

I cannot trust you within this nest,
like a songbird facing down a cuckoo,
with vulnerable chicks beneath my wings.
So I will batter and buffet for them
in defense of those I love,
until my soothing song has become
the hoarse cawing of the victorious
and you are only scattered feathers.

Waves and Shells

I remember forever summers, days of ocean depth
fathomless and rich with mysteries to explore,
submerged for eternities in the seeming vastness
spanning the gulf of Time called childhood.

I am not grey now, but know well it comes
faster and faster with each distracted moment:
like minnows, the days flash silver by,
almost nothing in my shallow tidepool weeks.

Is it merely aging perception, I wonder,
or does the changing of childish whimsy
shorten the coursing nature of each second
and send them scattering in schools?

Yet I find myself caught in waves again,
cresting and crashing into deeper currents
in moments so painful they stand outside
of Time, a sea unto themselves.

I cannot escape the fact the surf is seldom
the kind of joyous occasion one would wish,
but instead tempestuous storms stretching on,
forcing the mind to focus on the now.

But it is the constant presence of suffering
which offers meaning to the brighter shallows,
like waves rolling endlessly upon the beach,
leaving behind fragile, beautiful shells.

Autumn Reminder

I feel it stirring in the changing of the leaves,
the saturnine mood huddled under dripping eaves—
a bittersweet recollection: all things pass away,
even joys we clutch tightly, hoping they will stay.

Wherein lies the sweetness there, one may ask,
when the thoughts themselves in sorrow bask?
It is the fortune one tasted the sweetness at all,
those feathers of light which from fragile wings fall.

I do not begrudge the melancholia of this season,
for such reminders come with divine reason.
Hope does not spring from certain times, you see:
it clings like the promise of a yellow leaf to a tree.

If all things are ephemeral, so too is sorrow's face
and every passing sunbeam will have its place.
One cannot know a coin's single side sans opposite,
and expect to be of its true value cognizant.

A Post Mortem

An anatomy of the things you were at thirteen,
or perhaps more correctly, a post mortem:

Sensitive as a weathervane to winds of emotion around you,
is it any wonder you had to make peace to find peace in yourself?
So engrossed by worlds of imagination and flights of fancy,
you would read in every quiet moment and scribble wishes in
margins.
Uprooted as a sapling and replanted in unfamiliar soil,
lonely you, locked in the solitary confinement of peripheries.
So certain of a future you wanted in service and duty like Mom,
craving meaning and belonging as a part of bigger things.
You wandered outdoors making up stories or played soccer
with the few people you were brave enough to approach.
So much of it then was playing pretend even before
the specter of Death came and darkened your door.

An anatomy of things you were at sixteen,
or perhaps more correctly, a post mortem:

A mind as sharp as the razorblades turned on your own flesh,
winning arguments in debate class as a sort of ceramic mask.
You craved approval from the adults around you in school,
though half your essays were late and tear-stained.

And the friends who you'd managed to make, you always kept
well at arm's length in case they noticed something was wrong.
So certain of that first love you felt for your childhood friend,
never thinking that in a few years it'd be burning itself to the
ground.
You stayed up late on weekends to made up games and stories,
because playing a character was easier than talking as yourself.
So much of it then was playing pretend even after
the specter of Death came and built himself a home.

An anatomy of things you were at twenty-one,
or perhaps more correctly, a post mortem:

You struggled so hard against the buffeting storms of emotions,
how could it be a surprise that you felt without a center?
You needed to excel in classes just to prove to yourself
something inside was worth keeping alive another day.
But strangling secrets had already dug roots so deep down,
not even a 4.0 could save you from self-starvation.
And to the person you wanted to love you the most,
you didn't have the words to admit that something was wrong.
He'd talk about future and you'd nod along numbly,
because you wouldn't see even five minutes in front of your nose.
So much of it then was playing pretend, especially after
the specter of Death had made off with your sense of self.

And now where you're standing on an island built out of sand,
age twenty-nine, but still in so many ways caught like a rat in a
trap:

SONGS OF RECOVERY

post mortem, at thirteen, at sixteen, at twenty-one...

Heartbeats

My heart does not skip beats at your arrival;
instead, it slows to calm under your words' balm,
because it knows it has found a place to belong.

My heart does not sing like a bird on wing,
but huddles and hums with a quieter joy,
because intimacy means more than infatuation.

My heart does not leap like a bullfighter's pulse;
instead, it spins me up in a silken cocoon,
where it is only you and I for the afternoon.

My heart does not look forward or back,
but sinks into the moment like roots,
finding connection amidst the uncertainty.

My heart does not cling to promises forever;
instead, it takes moments as something savored,
to be cherished when they are no more.

I know, for you, my love is a cracked pearl,
a flawed gem, filled with mortal shortcomings,
but it is still given from the bottom of my heart.

Love Letters

I keep no count of syllables or words
to confine the letters I write you
for when you are old enough to understand.
Instead, I scribble until my ballpoints break
and the shoebox lids no longer fit.
I pour out rivers of affection
and oceans of hope,
as if from an ever-flowing inkwell.

I cannot breathe life into the dead,
but I will write you stories of your father
from the childhood we shared,
and I will carry the pride of two
to shower down on all you do
when others let things fade into silence.
Although I am far from you now,
my thoughts do not stray from you
nor all the tribulations you face.

I wish I could lift you into the sky
and spin you until my arms are tired
and say how much you've grown,
how happy I am to see you,
how lucky I am to be with you,

but Life makes small my hopes and I.

So let this epigraph be your future:
may you never know a love with conditions,
may your challenges teach you growth,
may your friendships flourish like dandelions
with dreams carried far and wide,
may you find wholeness and humor
your most constant companions—
and when you open each envelope,
may you feel the connection and joy
I bequeath in trust with every tear
of distance I shed now.

With all my love,
Auntie

A Reflection of Home

The thrumming of a car over patchwork roads
sings a melody of welcome home more sweetly
than the crooning country coming across the radio.

This is the place of open sky, cradled by windswept peaks
capped in glittering white in winter months, to the delight
of skiers and snowshoers who traverse their slopes
until the bursting green of spring's sudden thaw,
when wildflowers adorn the mountain meadows all around.

Where amber pastureland studded with simple farmhouses,
or trailer homes dusty from their gravel drives,
like pebbles taken from the Missouri and set in place
as checkers on a board of gold and emerald,
wraps around our town.

Here, a daily commute becomes communion
with placid lakes, crystalline streams, and the ever-changing clouds,
where azure yields to rolling storms and thunderous awe in summer,
or falls to a frigid hush as autumn chills the air.

It is a lake of golden lights too few at night

to truly dim the panoply of glimmering constellations,
surrounded on all sides by shores of shadows,
where no illumination save occasional headlights pierces forest
highways.

Here, wilderness intersects with slow-growing progress,
from city deer to barn owls to coyotes who dare to run
along grey fencelines despite old neighbor ladies
who would gladly discourage them with a rifle,
to protect curious cattle kept off the interstate
by the guards that rattle beneath truck tires.

Small town coffee-shops offer community so easily,
at least until the sidewalks all but roll up at seven,
when we sleepy-eyed night owls cluster around
our formica tables at Shellie's Cafe,
open so mercifully for all twenty-four hours of the day.
Restaurants serve as little hubs for neighbors and friends
to reconnect in all those taken-for-granted ways.
It doesn't matter if the staff know your name,
since they'll smile and ask with a pop quiz about your day.

A comfortable contradiction exists in different grandeurs
visible on the shaded streets charitably called "downtown",
where sometimes heavy rains remind once it was
a simple gold miner's running, last-chance gulch.

First and foremost, the sun-drenched spires
of red tiles and sweetly tolling bells topping

soaring St. Helena's Cathedral,
its interior all in white marble with a golden sacristy
and breathtaking stained glass windows worthy
of some medieval kingly patron, so detailed
their expressions seem alive, caught in reverence,
and their halos beaten gold that gleams holy
in the hushed candelight of Good Friday Mass,
or reflect triumphant in the resounding song
of the pipe organ playing Handel's Messiah.

Not far is the minaret of the Civic Center
built by the Shriners in an almost Andalusian style,
home to the Symphony and Fire Department alike,
with endless activities beside where the farmer's market
and Alive at Five celebrate the fleeting summer.

Too, from downtown, one can see the brickwork,
more than a century old, of Carroll College—
but also the aged wooden Firetower which stands
an unceasing watch over the Gulch from its overlook,
vigilant on Mount Helena's verdant, craggy slopes:
a peak, like the Sleeping Giant, visible from all the valley.

If one takes the time to wander down the brick paths
of Reeder's Alley, still preserved for a century and a half
by the people who love it so,
down into the Walking Mall with its statues,
almost spontaneous murals and chalk art,
one comes to find an intersection between

weathered past and vibrantly hopeful future.

It is visible in children playing chess with giant pieces
outside the storefront for Martin's Wines,
in a library that has leaned into difficult times,
and further down, in a rainbow-fronted bookstore
where signs promise you, whoever you are,
are loved for the difference that you are.
It is visible in the Holter Museum, where local art
is displayed for a donation box, not a fee—
where Our Place, for those struggling with addiction's demons,
and God's Love offers shelter to those without,
while the Food Share eases the pain of deprivation
hand in hand with community gardens—
all these offer little breaths of hope.

There are many patchwork imperfections here,
in the streets which sometimes make no sense
and the people who close themselves off to others,
and the cracks that swallow souls so easily,
when what they needed was a gentle catch.
But even in those moments of opinionated quarrel
or heartwrenching privation and pain,
one remembers the thrumming melody
sung by a car over many a patched pothole
and the rhythmic rattling of driving back dirt roads.

In a place where opposites meet,
wilderness butting up against settled spaces

or beauty flourishing beside broken things,
there are bound to be cracks and gaps.
What I have found here, what I hope flourishes
in every place a human could call home,
is the desire and willingness to mend.

I remember my hometown for its hiking trails,
its simple pleasures, its brewhouses and cafes,
its new beginnings for so many,
its living, breathing memories,
but most of all for its people, the menders,
who have so often been Kindness itself.

A Labor of Love

I have found such extraordinary love
in such ordinary places, as if
sapphires scattered all across the sidewalk:
in pealing giggles, laugh lines, aching tears,
and the quiet balm for emptiness called,
for lack of a greater word, companionship.
It flourishes here without a how or why,
except, perhaps, "You were you."

We made together a haven for hurting hearts,
a sanctuary in an office complex,
with sunlit windows for the doctors,
and gorgeous pictures for us—
the greatest of them a simple yard sign
held to the wall with stolen gorilla tape,
which reads, "YOU ARE LOVED."
All this, a place where I healed as much
as the patients who walked through
our ever-creaking door into
our home away from home.

I wonder if you know, o gemstones,
the magnitude of light refracted by your facets,
casting sunbeams into shadowed chasms

where despair and desolation feed.
So many times have I stumbled darkly,
feeling with numb fingers for a lifeline
while all the devils of my mind knocked below—
only to have your gentle light illuminate
the path back to the world above.

If we are reflections of divinity and grace,
perfection and adoration in the flawless sense,
imprinted finitely in the mold of something infinite,
nowhere have I seen that glimmer brighter
than when it shines in your everyday words
of kindness, tumbling like afterthoughts,
without want for anything in return—
except, perhaps, for everyone to feel enough...
or failing that, "a million dollars and margaritas".

Gravity and Milkweed

There is a gravity holding all things in their course,
as inexorable as the moon's pull on the tide,
as irresistible as the sun's warmth on fragile leaves—
I feel it in my chest every time you leave me,
drawing me along in your wake,
a fish hooked on spinner by an absent angler.

Love is not brought into being in an instant:
instead, it grows like milkweed up through cracks
in the stony shell around my heart,
giving sustenance to butterfly longings.

I did not know it bloomed as year followed year,
even as we spoke of growth and gardening.
Now I do not know how to hold the sea of emerald
and delicate pink that has supplanted my shell,
for it seems the best I can do is press lips to petals,
and hope someday the roots which bind find home.

Love is not brought into being by choice,
but it turns me to follow your voice's echoes—
as waves surge to shore urged by celestial silver,
as sunflowers track Helios's chariot in the sky.

And though you know the change you made in me,
you do not hear what is etched on my soul
when I mouth the words, "I love you."

Yet here I remain with you as a friend,
and I would not trade that time for the world itself.

Tending Wounds

The burning abrasions you leave on your flesh
scorch my heart to ashes as I watch,
unable to act, except to taste the bitterness of tears.

You tell me, "Go away. I don't want you to see this."
I stay, with antibiotic cream and bandages
and hospital tape that never holds for long.

I want to scream for you to believe me,
as I tend wounds and let you spit out your hurt,
that you deserve a life of happiness and peace.

It aches in old wounds long scarred over
to see the angry crimson of bloody scrapes,
and in my throat, where the lump of sorrow forms.

You have such a marvelous mind, clever wit,
caring heart, powerful voice, strong spirit—
but you cling to this demon and cannot know them.

My arm around your shaking shoulders does little,
except remind you that you are not alone,
but I wonder sometimes if you even feel its presence.

SONGS OF RECOVERY

If all I can do is be there with bandages and soft words,
for the scant, fleeting time you are under my care,
I will do it and hope my comfort can soothe.

For your sake, though, I wish with all my heart
you could borrow my vision just for a moment,
and see yourself as you are, deserving of
so much better, so much more.

Valentine Thoughts

When I think of this day,
I think of love letters yet unsent,
Those tremulous daydreams etched
onto paper with the intoxicating ink of hope.

When I think of this day,
I think not of candy and childish cards,
but the soft beat of your pulse
as it flutters under my fingertips.

When I think of this day,
I think of all the promises lovers make:
the forever, the only, the dearest secret things,
and a longing to whisper them all to you.

When I think of this day,
I think not of endings or beginnings.
Instead, there is simply this in present tense:
the gift of spending my hours with you.

Dragon Slayer

We are told to seek out true love's kiss
and brave knights in shining armor,
because here, in the world, dragons roam
the difficult mountains of our lives,
and every girl is a princess,
waiting as a prize for a savior.

And I think perhaps I have found myself
something entirely different than a dragonslayer.

When the reptilian eyes of envy settle
upon me and chill my bones to freezing,
it is your hand that steadies my shoulder.
When the fire surges down in waves
I do not think I can withstand,
it is your voice that reminds me of my shield.

When my hands shake because I hurt
and I do not think it is in me to slay the beast,
I feel your grip around my fingers,
holding my sword to my hand,
and then love comes as a simple reminder:
"Of course you can do this."

K. OLSEN

My life has many dragons to vanquish,
each a battle harder fought than the last
until I am beaten and bloody and bowed.
So often I do not think I can continue,
yet you are there whispering, "I have faith in you."

Your life has many dragons to vanquish,
each a vicious monster lurking in mental shadows,
no less intolerable and difficult than my own,
and when you stumble, I catch you in my arms,
because I see all of hope and trust in you.

I am not your prize, nor are you my knight,
and neither of us wear armor gleaming in the sun,
but when the dragons press all around,
my back meets yours and I feel safe,
because I know we can do this together—where none could
alone.

Thank You Notes

Christine, a brief note of appreciation, as we are blind
To our own good, as the eye can't see itself:

You have a gift for meeting people where they travel
and without judgment, walking alongside them:
offering them shelter from inclement weathers
and the respite from an isolation few can breach.

I cannot imagine having come so far without
the companionship and wisdom that you offer,
the clarity of kindness translated into right action,
and the comfort you give born of understanding.

I am fortunate to know you and so are your patients,
even if you may not see the scope of your safe harbor,
or the way we know you advocate for our wellbeing.

Thank you for everything you do.

K. OLSEN

Nancy, a brief note of appreciation, as we are blind
To our own good, as the eye can't see itself:

I think you do not know the measure of your good:
the sincerity flowing from you like spring water,
enabling all sweet things to flourish in a wasteland,
because you care so genuinely where many do not.

I cannot thank you enough for all the moments
where you have said, "I don't know, but I am here",
approaching with waves of curious compassion,
the best antidote to the isolating drought of pain

I am fortunate to know you and so are your patients,
even if you think you never say quite the right thing
because truthfully, you do, and have the perfect hug.

Thank you for everything you do.

SONGS OF RECOVERY

Anne, a brief note of appreciation, as we are blind
To our own good, as the eye can't see itself:

There is such a centering to your presence,
a calming grounding to the way that you care,
which takes the hearts of all those who suffer
and gathers them safely away from cruel winds.

I wish you could see how people open up, relieved,
when you listen with such authenticity and intent
that they realize they are someone who matters,
and little by little, the healing creeps its way in.

I am fortunate to know you and so are your patients,
even if your extraordinary grace seems ordinary to you
as you extend it so effortlessly.

Thank you for everything you do.

K. OLSEN

Mark, a brief note of appreciation, as we are blind
To our own good, as the eye can't see itself:

I have seen in you the healing power of laughter,
which blooms in dark times fields of tender mercies
as you step out of your office like a sunbeam,
lifting spirits with such ease despite your own grief.

It is rare to find anyone who believes so fiercely
that everyone can be redeemed and brought up
into the light with just respect and persistence,
yet you practice daily what the best preach.

I am fortunate to know you and so are your patients,
even if you cannot see your light for its glow
or realize the shadows shrink with your passing.

Thank you for everything you do.

SONGS OF RECOVERY

Andrea, a brief note of appreciation, as we are blind
To our own good, as the eye can't see itself:

You move through the world with such tenderness,
a gardener coaxing downtrodden plants to bloom,
and so healing follows in your wake like flowers,
after a forest fire, turn their faces towards the dawn.

The people and animals who flourish because
of the gentleness and patience you show them
extend endlessly in echoes through eternity,
each one improved because of your example.

I am fortunate to know you and so are your patients,
even if the scope of the garden is hidden
by its own bright leaves and effervescent blooms.

Thank you for everything you do.

K. OLSEN

Bridgid, a brief note of appreciation, as we are blind
To our own good, as the eye can't see itself:

You touch people's hearts with such merciful skill
and benevolence that makes pain seem lessened,
if only because in your office, it is shared
with an empathy that few can even comprehend.

In the changes for the better, I see your fingerprints
indelible upon the heart like an angel's feathers
graven like peace into grief-stricken stone;
and in the worst, I see a flickering of hope.

I am fortunate to know you and so are your patients,
even if you walk so lightly you never realize
the tracks of meaning and inspiration you leave behind.

Thank you for everything you do.

For K—

You are rarer than you know,
a patient beach-comber who walks the sands,
searching for troubled souls washed ashore
like splintered sand dollars and shattered shells.

It takes a seldom-found compassion and grace
to gather each piece by carefully sieving sand,
and then with the softest, but firm touches,
apply the glue of faith to mend their cracks.

Like kintsugi pottery, the warmth you give
lingers in the people you have touched:
golden transmutation of scars into strengths
more beautiful because of your beholding eye.

Your words make plain the possibility of healing.
Your actions encourage it with every brush.
Your trust gives those who come to you faithless
a chance to find their own value as greater
than the sum of merely their parts.

How do I know this to be true,
with all the certainty a soul can hold?
Because I have been at times the shards of shell

fortunate enough to pass through your hands,
and I am immeasurably better for it.

Briar-Sting

How is it you are always further,
the closer I begin to feel?
I feel like I am chasing my own shadow
with embracing arms and tearful eyes,
crashing through the briars
and wondering, "Why does it sting so much?"

Surely there is only one world,
and yet somehow we stand in two,
and though the 'twain may meet,
never may they cross or mingle—
such that I am standing on one shore
of this rushing, nonsense reality
and you stand upon its opposite.

What are words for a bridge,
when love strikes my reason dumb
and deafer still you seem
to what ardor my muted self allows?
Is this punishment for sins of callow youth,
inflicted blindly and well-meaning on others
when it was first my season to love?

I ask again, uncomprehending,

for my heart is a foolish thing,
incapable of turning from you
or doing anything aside from loving more:
why does it sting so much?

How It Flies

How strange a thing, time.
Some moments seem everlasting,
others agonizingly ephemeral,
all the sum parts of our raptures and sorrows alike
flying away, away, like the arrow of Fate
loosed by our fingers into eternity.

How short a thing, time.
The measure of a man, barely the blink of an eye,
and the growth of a mountain range
is nothing compared to the lifespan of a star.
It is a *seeming* thing, shifting and changing,
even as it flows on like a river
whose course cannot be turned back.

How precious a thing, time.
Everyone grasps for it,
some spend and some squander,
but no one ever has enough:
so many vital things left unsaid, undone,
for the sake of the monotonous tick of obligation,
until only an empty hourglass remains.

And so I etch myself words in my glass heart,

fearing not its breakage, but its neglect.
Remember to share my gratitudes.
Remember to be kind and patient.
Remember to be humble and forgiving.
Remember to apportion space for others.
Remember it is not a race to win.
Remember feast and famine alike come and go.

Remember that nothing is permanent,
and all things are ever-changing,
for time waits for no one—
already it is gone:
tempus fugit, memento mori.

Sweet Relief

What sweet relief a feeling is!

I keep my sorrows bundled to my breast,
and kiss them close with tenderness.
I heed my furies when they screech and scream,
divine-sent heralds warning of unjust things.
I clasp each fleeting joy to my fondest heart,
and leave them room enough to depart.
I treasure every moment with fiery love,
and bank the embers of its loss.

I comfort each anxiety with welcoming arms,
beckoning them to sit around my sides.
I lay out palms for pride and guilt,
as I know for them my life is built.
I offer trust and confidence to fear itself,
as easily as places perched beside my hearth.
I swing hopes high as they wish in my hands,
as if little children clambering for stars.
I make space for disappointments and grief,
ushering in old friends come to visit me.

For each one carries a piece of the human soul
and offers a part to sum greater than the whole.

I tell you, for all the gold in all the world,
all precious stones, all laurels, all crowns—
I would not trade their wisdom or their need,
for they know best how to heal me.

What sweet relief a feeling is,
when you have known the numbing of nothingness!

Also by K. Olsen

The Revealed World
Beneath the Iron
Heart of Flame

Standalone
Daydreams From The Ashes
Songs of Recovery